HAM HOUSE

MAURICE TOMLIN

A NATIONAL TRUST PROPERTY
ADMINISTERED BY
THE VICTORIA AND ALBERT MUSEUM

THIS GUIDE IS SPONSORED BY **Mobil**

VICTORIA AND ALBERT MUSEUM

PUBLISHED BY THE VICTORIA AND ALBERT MUSEUM, 1986
© THE TRUSTEES OF THE V&A
DESIGN BY LAURENCE BRADBURY DESIGN ASSOCIATES
PRINTED IN GREAT BRITAIN BY JOLLY & BARBER LTD, RUGBY
ISBN 0 948107 49 9

Front cover: The Cloisters
Inside front cover/half title: Late 19th-century
view of the house
Title page: The South Front from the Wilderness
Back cover: Ham House seen from the entrance drive.

CONTENTS

Elizabeth, Countess of Dysart, in her Youth. By Lely.

FOREWORD

Ham House is remarkable because it presents us with more aspects of 17th-century life than any other house in the country.

Apart from the fact that its architectural fabric has been preserved virtually unchanged since the 1670s (when the building was enlarged and re-organized by the Duke and Duchess of Lauderdale), it still contains all its furnishings from that period – and that is a most exceptional phenomenon. Moreover, the gardens have been so little altered since then that it has been possible to restore them to their original guise.

As a result, we can still obtain a clear impression of this house as a complete entity, the grounds constituting an ordered extension of the house and its carefully planned interior.

Ancient houses reveal themselves only gradually. As we study them more and our fund of information is built up, so our understanding of their significance and complexity deepens and changes. There is no finality in these matters; thus the arrangements of the rooms at Ham House are continually being adjusted, always, we hope, the better to convey the intentions and aspirations of the Lauderdales and Dysarts, their architects and decorators. For we believe it is into such matters that many of those who visit our 'stately homes' seek an insight, and there is nowhere that they can do so better than at Ham House.

Each successive edition of the guidebook summarizes the current state of our knowledge as it pertains to this particular house – indeed, a reading of the various editions will one day reveal much about changing attitudes to the presentation of country houses, which springs from the rapidly growing interest that has become increasingly apparent since the War. The several inventories of the house were published in 1980 by the Furniture History Society, with commentaries by Peter Thornton and Maurice Tomlin, under the title, *The Furnishing and Decoration of Ham House*. The visitor who wishes to study the interior arrangements of this important house in greater detail may care to refer to this. A brief bibliography of other recent work is given at the end.

This new publication is divided into two sections – a tour of the house to be used by visitors as they go round and a history of the house in which the phases are dealt with chronologically.

The house is today presented as far as possible as it was in the 17th century with stress being laid on the Lauderdale period of the 1670s. Visitors view the rooms in the sequence intended at the time. For example, one enters the State Apartment from the Great Stairs and passes through the sequence of rooms to the State Bedchamber – the culmination of the sequence – and the Queen's Closet. One then retreats back through the whole sequence, as one would have done when the rooms were new, and one should then get a better impression of how such a house actually worked.

A few items of furniture have been lent to the house from the collection at the Victoria and Albert Museum in order to complete the furnishing of certain rooms. An asterisk has been added where such pieces are mentioned in this guide.

Where the original wall-hangings, window-curtains and chair-covers have not survived, modern reproductions have been provided.

The House and its gardens were generously given to the National Trust in 1948 by the late Sir

Lyonel Tollemache, Bt, and his son, Mr Cecil Tollemache, whose ancestors had inhabited the house for three centuries. To ensure proper maintenance of the property, the National Trust made it over on a long lease to the Ministry of Works (now the Department of the Environment), while the contents were purchased by the Government and entrusted to the care of the Victoria and Albert Museum, which is responsible for the administration of the house. We are much indebted to Major-General Sir Humphry Tollemache, C.B., C.B.E., D.L., for allowing us to quote from the building accounts of the 1670s, which are among his family papers.

John Morley,
Keeper, Department of Furniture and Interior Design.

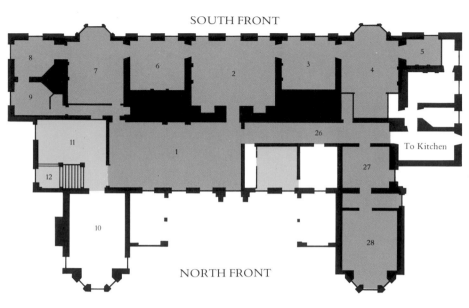

SOUTH FRONT

NORTH FRONT

The colour coding indicates the
period of the principal
decorative features of the
rooms.

Early C17

1670's

Early C19

To Kitchen

GROUND FLOOR
1 Great Hall
2 Marble Dining Room
3 Duke's Dressing Room
4 Duchess's Bedchamber

5 Duke's Closet
6 Withdrawing Room
7 Yellow Bedchamber or
Volury Room
8 White Closet

9 Duchess's Private Closet
10 Chapel
11 Inner Hall
12 Great Staircase
26 West Passage

27 Gentlemen's Dining Room
28 Back Parlour

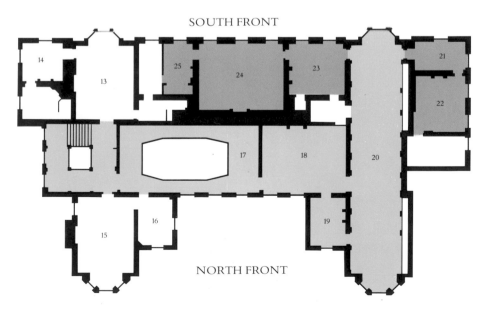

SOUTH FRONT

NORTH FRONT

FIRST FLOOR
13 Yellow Satin Room
14 Yellow Satin Dressing
Room

15 Room over the Chapel
(Museum Room)
16 Cabinet of Miniatures
17 Round Gallery
18 North Drawing Room

19 Green Closet
20 Long Gallery
21 Library Closet
22 Library

23 Antechamber to the
Queen's Bedchamber
24 Queen's Bedchamber
25 Queen's Closet

OUTLINE HISTORY

Ham House was built in 1610 by Sir Thomas Vavasour, Knight Marshal to James I. Considerable alterations to the interior, notably the building of the new Great Staircase, were made by William Murray, 1st Earl of Dysart, between 1637 and 1639. But the house as it appears today is largely the creation of his daughter, Elizabeth, and her second husband, the Duke of Lauderdale. During the 1670s, having employed the architect William Samwell to enlarge the house by adding a new suite of rooms along the South Front on each floor (see plans on p.9) they furnished the interior with a luxuriousness that was remarkable even in that lavish age. Much of the original furniture seems to have been stored away for long periods and consequently most of it still survives. Although the original window curtains and many of the wall-hangings no longer exist, the existence of detailed inventories has made it possible to recreate the interiors much as they would have been in the time of the Lauderdales. Ham House thus still presents much of its sumptuous 17th-century appearance and still vividly recalls the 'politer way of living' introduced after the Restoration, which 'soon passed to luxury and intolerable expense'.

The only significant alterations since the time of the Lauderdales were made by the 4th Earl of Dysart, who acquired some sumptuous new furniture shortly after inheriting the title in 1727 and was also responsible for some minor architectural alterations, which included the installation of the existing sash windows.

(For a more detailed history see p.90.)

Main Entrance doorway.

TOUR OF THE HOUSE

THE GREAT HALL

In the original H-shaped house of 1610 this room formed the horizontal bar in the letter 'H' and had a window on the right of the fireplace. The opening of the front door into one end of the Hall and the disposing of the service rooms at the other side show the surviving influence of the traditional mediaeval house-plan, where the entrance would have led into a screens passage at one end of the hall. The raised section of floor at the far end, however, is not a dais but merely marks the position of the wall at that end before the room was enlarged in the 1630s. The two figures, traditionally said to be William Murray, 1st Earl of Dysart, and his Countess, in the costumes of Mars and Minerva are attributed to Francesco Fanelli, a sculptor from the court circle of Charles I (active c. 1609–c. 1665), who may also have executed the gilded bronze mounts on the chimneypiece. The wall-panelling dates from the 1670s. Originally the ceiling continued right across, the octagonal opening probably having been made about 1690 (see p. 101).

Detail of chimneypiece in the Great Hall.

Furniture:
The oak hall-chairs, bearing the arms of the Tollemache family, were supplied by the firm of George Nix in 1730.

The Palladian-style mahogany side-tables are of similar date.

Paintings (clockwise from the left of the fireplace):
Lyonel Tollemache, 4th Earl of Dysart (1708–70) by John Vanderbank (1694–1739).

Grace Carteret, Countess of Dysart (1713–55) by John Vanderbank.

Charlotte Walpole, Countess of Dysart (1738–89) by Sir Joshua Reynolds (1723–92). Exhibited at the Royal Academy in 1775.

Louisa Manners, Countess of Dysart (1745–1840) by John Hoppner (1758–1810), after Reynolds. The original (exhibited at the Royal Academy in 1779) is now in the Iveagh Bequest at Kenwood.

Portrait of a Flemish Gentleman. Attributed to Pieter Pourbus (1523–84). Formerly identified as Sir Lyonel Tollemache (1562?–1621).

Henrietta Cavendish (d.1717. Wife of Lyonel, Lord Huntingtower, grandson of the Duchess of Lauderdale) by Sir Godfrey Kneller (1646–1723).

James Stuart, Duke of Lennox and Richmond (1612–55) after Sir Anthony Van Dyck (1599–1641). The original is in the Metropolitan Museum, New York. Called *The Marchioness of Winchester* (2nd wife of the 5th Marquess) after Van Dyck. The original has not been traced.

13

Great Hall.

THE MARBLE DINING ROOM

Used for dining on informal occasions, this is the central room of the extensions of the 1670s and from it the apartments of the Duke and Duchess of Lauderdale extend to either side in the typical formal plan adopted from Continental practice. It stands on the central axis of the grounds, which continues across the grass parterres, through the Wilderness to the South Gate and along the South Avenue to Ham Common.

The carving of the oak panelling was done by John Bullimore in 1672/73; for the *bunches of leaves about ye dores* he charged 2s. per foot. The original black and white marble floor as seen on the threshold, which gave the room its name, was replaced about 1756 by the present very fine parquetry floor. In that year the 4th Earl of Dysart acquired a *Sett of Gilt Leather Hangings White and Gold, Mosaic Pattern*, a description that clearly fits the present hangings. (A section of the original gilded leather hangings of the 1670s, richly decorated with cherubs, fruit and flowers, can be seen in the Museum Room.)

Left: Part of the original gilded leather wall-hangings.

Marble Dining Room.

Rose, the Royal Gardener, presenting Charles II with the first pineapple grown in England.
After Henry Danckerts (c.1625–c.1679)

Furniture:

The walnut caned chairs★ are arranged round the walls in a formal manner, as was the custom when they were not in use. In 1679 there were eighteen chairs of this type in the room.

The cedarwood side-tables of about 1675 were designed to stand in the alcoves. Below one of them is a marble wine-cooler.

The mid-17th century gate-leg table, of oak and pine, is one of three that stood in the recesses on the window wall in the 17th century.

The gilded pier-glasses date from about 1730.

The bracket clock★ is signed by Joseph Knibb.

Inset Paintings:

(Over the fireplace) *Rose, the Royal Gardener, presenting Charles II with the first pineapple grown in England*, after the painting attributed to Henry Danckerts (c.1625–c.1679) in the collection of the Marchioness of Cholmondeley at Houghton Hall. An inscription on the back states that it was copied by Thomas Hewart, aged twenty, in October 1787. (The house is an imaginary one but the formal garden may be compared with the somewhat similar layout at Ham.)

(Over the entrance doorway) *A Fantastic Landscape* by a follower of Hieronymus Bosch. Another version by the same artist, entitled *Christ Breaking Down the Doors of Hell*, is at Hampton Court Palace.

(Other insets) 17th-century copies of a series of playing boys by Polidoro Caldara (Roman School; d.1543), acquired by Charles I in 1637 and now at Hampton Court Palace.

Hanging Painting:

Cocks and Hens. Attributed to Frans Snyders (1579–1657).

Gilded pier-glass, c.1730.

The Duke's Dressing Room.

THE DUKE'S DRESSING ROOM

This room served as an antechamber to the adjoining bedchamber. The artificial graining of the panelling dates from the 1670s. The jib doors, as seen here, were for the use of servants. Most of the porcelain★ displayed in the house is Chinese, of the K'ang Hsi period (1662–1722).

Furniture:
The ebonised table and candlestands, carved in the auricular style, are believed to have been made in Holland about 1670.

Six caned armchairs are listed as having been here in 1679; the chair nearest the fireplace is the only original one to have survived.

The cabinet and side-table *en suite* are fine examples of floral marquetry in various woods and ivory. About 1680.

Inset paintings:
(Over fireplace) *A Battle-Piece* by Jan Wyck (1640–1702).

(Over doors) Two *Classical Landscapes* by Henry Danckerts (c.1625–c.1679). The one above the east door, signed and dated 1673, shows Giambologna's Appenino in the garden of the Villa at Pratolino near Florence.

Hanging paintings:
Saint Sebastian. Italian School.

Fra. Paolo Sarpi, historian of the Council of Trent. Artist unknown.

Ralph Wilbraham, brother of Grace Wilbraham, Countess of Dysart. Artist unknown; late 17th century.

Charles Maitland, 3rd Earl of Lauderdale (c.1620–91); brother of the Duke of Lauderdale. Artist unknown.

Sir Robert Worsley (1669–1747). Artist unknown; dated 1693.

19

THE DUCHESS'S BEDCHAMBER

This was the Duke's Bedchamber when the first alterations were made to the house in the 1670s, flanked by his Dressing Room and Closet. By 1675, however, the Duchess had taken it over, while he had moved to *her* old bedchamber (see p. 28) at the other end of the house. The reason for the move may have been her need for more extensive accommodation for her lady-in-waiting to the left of the alcove (not open to the public) and by the provision of a bathroom in the basement below.

The bill from the carver, John Bullimore, dated April 1673, includes an item for *33ft of great rafle leaves at 1s. 8d.* This was for the moulding framing the alcove.

Duchess's Bedchamber.

Strongbox with brass mounts, c.1675.

Furniture:

The bed is a modern reconstruction.

There were *thre arm'd Chairs carved & black & gilded* here in 1679.

The chairs seen here now are of this type but are in fact very remarkable reproductions made for the house in the early 19th century (c.f. those in the Yellow Satin Room, p.50).

The Duchess's *box with an extraordinary lock,* dating from about 1675, stands beside the fireplace; it is veneered with kingwood parquetry and the contemporary cabinet opposite is similarly decorated.

The brass-bound jewel-case also belonged to the Duchess but was supplied with a new stand in the 18th century.

The clock,★ signed *John Knibb, Oxon,* is similar to the one that stood here in the Duchess's time.

The pole-screen with silver mounts is an

Sea-piece by Willem van de Velde the Younger.

Elizabeth Dysart with her first husband, Sir Lyonel Tollemache, and her sister, Lady Maynard. Attributed to Joan Carlile.

early example (c.1675) of its type, though the tapestry panel is an 18th-century replacement.

The tongs and shovel are similarly mounted with silver; this silver chimney-furniture, which is a feature of several of the rooms, has long been a celebrated curiosity and strikingly testifies to the Lauderdales' luxurious taste. As John Evelyn (or his daughter, Mary) wrote:

> *The chimney furniture of plate*
> *For irons now quite out of date*
> *(Mundus Muliebris, or the Ladies' Dressing*
> *Room Unlock'd & her Toilet Spread,* 1690).

Most of the fireplaces have their original iron firebacks; the plain delftware tiles are also original.

Inset paintings:

Over the bed: the ceiling, painted in oil on canvas, is in the style of Antonio Verrio (1639?– 1707).

Over the doors: four *Sea-Pieces* by Willem van de Velde the Younger (1633–1707). Signed and dated 1673, they are fine examples of the work of one of the greatest marine painters. Having been painted before the Duke relinquished this room, they have distinctly masculine connotations.

Hanging paintings:

The Duke of Lauderdale, in crayons, by Edmund Ashfield (active c.1670–1700). Signed and dated 1674–5.

Elizabeth Dysart (later Duchess of Lauderdale) *with her first husband, Sir Lyonel Tollemache, and her sister, Lady Maynard.* Attributed to Joan Carlile (1606?–79), this is an unusually early example (c.1648) of a conversation piece painted in England. It was reframed in the 18th century.

Overleaf: Duke's Closet.

23

THE DUKE'S CLOSET

The closet was a richly decorated little room, to which its owner could retire for privacy or into which his close friends or political associates might be invited.

Furniture:
The walnut armchair with partial gilding dates from about 1685. (In the 1670s there were a *Sleeping Chayre*, standing under a canopy, and two side chairs.)

The remarkable writing-cabinet, veneered with burr elm and ebony and embellished with silver mounts, was described in 1679 as a *scriptor garnished with silver*; traces of silvering can be seen on the legs of the stand.

Inset paintings:
Over the fireplace: *An Alchemist* signed Thomas Wyck (1616–77).

Below this: *A Sea-Piece* assigned to Van de Velde in the 1683 inventory.

The ceiling, painted in oil on plaster: *Two Female Figures representing Music* in the style of Antonio Verrio.

Hanging paintings:
Charles Maitland, 3rd Earl of Lauderdale by David Paton (worked c.1660–1695. Indian Ink).

Sir Thomas Delves, Bart. (1630–1713) attributed to Mary Beale (1632–97).

St Anthony. Italian School.

Head of Erasmus. Artist unknown.

Head of an Old Man by Gerard Dou (1613–75).

The frames of these two small portraits are carved in the style of Grinling Gibbons.

Returning through the Marble Dining Room, the visitor reaches:

24

THE WITHDRAWING ROOM

This room, to which one withdrew after a meal in the Marble Dining Room, also served as an ante-chamber to the adjoining bedchamber.

Furniture:
Pier-glass, table and stands, decorated with sections of incised Oriental lacquer; about 1675. (Bases of tables and stands renewed at a later date.)

Table decorated with European imitation of incised lacquer. Probably Dutch; about 1679.

Armchair, walnut with partial gilding; about 1685.

Table, kingwood; about 1675.

Pair of armchairs, ebonised and partly gilded; about 1680. (Part of the set from the adjoining bedchamber.)

Inset paintings:
Over the doors: Two more copies of the Polidoros at Hampton Court.

Over the fireplace: *Plants, Insects and a Squirrel* by A.C. Bega (1637–97).

Hanging paintings:
The Gathering of Manna. School of Bassano. (Reframed c.1736).

Hagar and Ishmael, after P.F. Mola (1612–66).

Charles I on Horseback, after Van Dyck. (Reframed in the late 18th century.)

Daniel in the Lion's Den, attributed to Jacopo Bassano (1510–92). Venetian School. (Reframed c.1736.)

The Passage of the Red Sea, signed by Jakob de Wett (1610–after 1671), a pupil of Rembrandt. (Reframed c.1736.)

Hagar and Ishmael, after P.F. Mola.

Withdrawing Room.

THE YELLOW BEDCHAMBER OR VOLURY ROOM

In an inventory drawn up about 1654 this was referred to as being the bedroom of Elizabeth Dysart (later Duchess of Lauderdale). The *black & yellow vain'd chimney in my Lady's Chamber* was installed by the mason, John Lampen, in 1672 at a cost of £15. By 1677 the room had come to be called the Yellow Bedchamber as it then had yellow damask wall hangings; at about this time the Duchess moved to the bedroom at the other end of the South Front and the Duke apparently took over this room until his death in 1682. According to an inventory drawn up in the following year, the bed had been removed and the room was now called the *Volury Roome*. (The word is apparently derived from the French *voliére* or *volerie*; bird-cages are known to have been built outside the bay windows and these in fact survived into the 1930s.)

In spite of her change-over to the bedroom at the other end of the house, the Duchess still retained her two closets adjoining her former bedchamber, in the same way as the Duke kept his ancillary rooms – seemingly a somewhat awkward arrangement.

28

Volury.

Left: Cabinet, probably made in Antwerp in the 1630s. *Above:* Detail of the cabinet on opposite page.

Furniture:

The bed, which comes from another room, still has some of the original material on the dome and finial and this colour scheme has governed the restoration of the whole room, which now has hangings and chair-covers *en suite*, as they would have been in the 17th century; the colours of this room in 1679 were in fact yellow and blue.

The chairs, of about 1680, are part of a set of ten that were in the room. (Two are now shown in the Withdrawing Room next door.)

The cabinet, probably made in Antwerp in the 1630s, is decorated with red tortoiseshell and has an elaborate architectural interior.

The gilded pier-glasses and console-tables date from the mid-18th century.

Inset paintings:

Two paintings of birds by Francis Barlow (1626?–1702), well known for his drawings and paintings of wild life; one is signed and dated 1673. These paintings, which are more appropriate for a lady's bedchamber, were installed when the room was still occupied by the Duchess.

Hanging paintings:

John Maitland, 1st Earl of Lauderdale (d.1645); father of the Duke of Lauderdale. Artist unknown.

An Alchemist by Thomas Wyck (1616–77).

A Battle Scene by Peter Tillemans (1684–1734).

Faun and Bacchante after Rubens. (Reframed c.1738.)

A Mediterranean Seaport by Thomas Wyck.

33

Pier-glass and console-table, c.1740.

THE WHITE CLOSET

This richly decorated little room and the Private Closet beyond formed part of the Duchess's original apartment and were retained by her. This closet was largely for show and was decorated in the most advanced taste; the corner chimneypiece was a notable innovation and the original windows and door to the garden were double-glazed.

South Front enfilade, seen from the White Closet.

White Closet.

Scriptor and chair in the White Closet.

Furniture:

Writing-cabinet or scriptor, decorated with kingwood oysterwork veneer and embossed silver mounts: about 1680.

The japanned chair, of about 1675, is designed in a naive attempt to reproduce an Oriental form. On its cresting is a coronet and the cypher ED (for Elizabeth Dysart). Unlike most late 17th-century chairs, it is decorated behind, suggesting that these chairs were grouped informally, rather than placed around the walls of the room as was customary. No doubt they were often used for the fashionable pastime of tea-drinking, for which their Oriental appearance would have been particularly appropriate. (In 1679 there was an *Indian furnace for tee garnish'd wt silver* in the room.)

The bronze bust of the Duchess's mother, Catherine Bruce, Countess of Dysart, retains its original gilding. Attributed to Francesco Fanelli; about 1640.

Inset paintings:

Ceiling: *Wisdom presiding over the Liberal Arts* by Verrio.

Chimneypiece: *Ham House from the South*, attributed to Henry Danckerts. This shows the formal garden very clearly.

Overdoors: *Italianate Landscapes* by Dirck van den Bergen (1640–95), one portraying Mercury and Battus from Ovid's *Metamorphoses*.

Hanging paintings:

Portrait of a Youth aged 18 in 1546. Italian School.

Head of St Paul by Benedetto Gennari (1633–1715).

Wooded Landscape possibly by Jan Wynants (c.1625–84).

The Holy Family by David Paton, after Andrea del Sarto.

Sir John Maitland, 1st Baron Maitland of Thirlestane (1545?–95) by Paton.

Virgin and Child with St John by Paton, after Raphael.

37

Ceiling of the White Closet by Verrio.

Japanned chair, c.1675.

THE DUCHESS'S PRIVATE CLOSET

The lowness of the entrance doorway, designed as a jib door on the other side, suggests that this little room had at first been intended for the lady-in-waiting and was only later converted by the Duchess into a richly-decorated closet. The borders of the original hangings were embroidered, giving an even richer appearance. The grey and yellow colour scheme echoes the colours in the *trompe l'oeil* ceiling, where the painted surrounds in turn imitate the marble of the chimneypiece.

Furniture:
The japanned chairs form part of the set of *Six Japan'd backstools with Cane bottomes* that the Duchess kept in this room.

The scriptor, of about 1675, is decorated with kingwood parquetry. (The artificial graining of the wall panelling may have been an attempt to imitate its figuring.)

The Javanese lacquer tea-table of similar date had a lower stage added in this country.

The miniature cabinet decorated with Chinese incised lacquer may well be the *Japan box for Sweetmeats and tea* that the Duchess kept here.

Duchess's Private Closet.

Ceiling of the Duchess's Private Closet by Verrio.

Inset paintings:
Classical Ruins and *A Sorceress among Classical Ruins*, both by William Gowe Ferguson (1632/3– after 1695).

The ceiling painting depicting Fortitude surrounded by figures symbolizing Time, Death and Eternity is attributed to Verrio.

Hanging paintings:
In 1679 the walls were hung with 23 pictures, mostly miniatures or small paintings. Among them were the following:

The Baptism of Christ by Abraham Bloemart (1564–c.1651). Dutch School.

(On the scriptor) *Catherine Bruce, Countess of Dysart* by John Hoskins (d.1664). Signed and dated 1638.

A West Indian Plantation by Franz Post (c.1612–80).

Peasant with a Jug. School of Teniers.

The other three seen here now are 18th-century fan paintings.

Catherine Bruce, Countess of Dysart, by John Hoskins.

41

THE CHAPEL

This was created by the Lauderdales from a room that had previously been the main Parlour (i.e. living room). The furniture and carved details were supplied by the joiner, Henry Harlow, in 1673 and 1674. The altar cloth of *crimson velvet & gould & silver stuff with gould & silver fringe* still drapes the original table; such coverings are now of the utmost rarity. The alms dish and candlesticks,★ of Flemish origin, are of a form commonly used on the altar in Anglican churches at that time.

42

The Chapel.

THE INNER HALL

Furniture:
The mahogany chairs date from about 1760.

Paintings:
*William, 2nd Duke of Hamilton, with the Earl
(later Duke) of Lauderdale* by Cornelius Johnson
(1593–1664?). Signed and dated 1649. A replica
is at Lennoxlove in the collection of the Duke
of Hamilton. Born in London of Flemish stock,
Johnson painted many striking English portraits
between 1620 and 1643, then withdrew to
Holland to avoid the Civil War. The two sitters
were in Holland with Charles II in 1649.

The Angel appearing to the Shepherds after
Abraham Bloemart (1564–c.1651).

The Battle of Lepanto, attributed to Cornelius
Vroom (1590/1–1661). Dutch School. Formerly
in the collection of Charles I.

A Blackbird with Cherries. Signed A.
Bosschaert.

44

The Battle of Lepanto by Cornelius Vroom (1590/1–1661).

Inner Hall and Great Staircase.

THE GREAT STAIRCASE

Constructed in 1637 or 1638, this handsome staircase is an early example of a type which reached its fullest development after the Restoration – a staircase in which the balustrade is composed of carved and pierced panels instead of balusters. In the earliest of such staircases, dating from towards the end of James I's reign, the panels are pierced with strapwork designs, while those constructed after the middle of the century are mostly ornamented with continuous scrollwork. The boldly carved trophies of arms at Ham are very unusual.

The bill of Thomas Carter, the joiner, includes items for making 'the great arch' between the Hall and the Staircase, for 24 yards of wainscot and for six windows and five doors and doorcases. There is no mention of the stairs themselves but a reference to the 'new great stairs' makes it clear that they were constructed at the same time. Mathew Goodricke, a decorative painter who worked for the Crown, painted and 'veined' the woodwork to imitate walnut and picked it out with gilding, while the plasterer, Joseph Kinsman, decorated the ceiling and soffits. The staircase was restored in 1980/81.

Panelling on the Great Staircase.

Panelling on the Great Staircase.

The Great Staircase. From S.C. Hall,
*Baronial Halls and Picturesque Edifices of
England,* 1848.

The landing on the Great Staircase.

Detail of doorway leading to the former Great Dining Room.

48

The paintings:

Landscape with Cattle by Dirk van den Bergen (1640–95). Signed D.V.B. Dutch School.

Diana with Nymphs by Adrian van Nieulandt (1587–1658). Signed and dated 1615. Dutch School.

Diana and Actaeon after an original by Titian in the Duke of Sutherland's collection.

Cupid, Mercury and Psyche after an original by Corregio formerly in Charles I's collection and now in the National Gallery.

Venus and a Satyr after the original by Titian in the Louvre.

Julius Caesar sending his Despatches to Rome by Jacob de Gheyn II (1565–1629).

Venus and Adonis after the original by Titian in the National Gallery.

Venus and the Organ Player after an original by Titian, formerly in Charles I's collection and now in the Prado, Madrid.

Doorways on the landing of the Great Staircase.

Detail of frieze in the Yellow Satin Room.

THE YELLOW SATIN ROOM
(LADY MAYNARD'S CHAMBER)

Margaret, Lady Maynard, the Duchess's sister, used this room from 1679 until her death in 1682. In the early 19th century it is believed to have been the bedroom of Louisa Manners, Countess of Dysart (1745–1840; see portrait). The present arrangement is based on the appearance of the room at that time, when it was furnished with the suite of furniture upholstered with yellow satin decorated with couched red cord and so became known as the Yellow Satin Room. The Jacobean-style frieze probably dates from the same time.

Furniture:

The bed is a modern reconstruction; the red cord trimmings have been remounted on modern silk.

The chairs (and also the stools and firescreen) were made in 1813, reproducing the design of a set of 17th-century chairs that may be seen downstairs but with their proportions slightly altered so that the early 18th-century covers could be used on them. (One of these covers – still unused – can be seen in the Museum Room.)

Armchair made in 1813 and covered with 18th-century material.

The very fine late 17th-century looking-glass, which closely resembles one at Windsor Castle, was here in the 19th century, as was the table *en suite*; the original candlestands belonging to the set have long since disappeared. The alabaster vases, probably North Italian, were in the Round Gallery in 1844.

The 18th-century lacquer chest was also listed as being in this room.

The square pianoforte in the form of a sofa-table is veneered with rosewood and amboyna. It was made by John Broadwood and Sons in 1801.

The dressing-box veneered with engraved ivory is Indian, 18th century.

The mid-18th century pier-glass bears the Tollemache crest of a winged horse.

Inset paintings:
Two *Landscapes with Cattle* by Dirck van den Bergen (1640–95).

Hanging paintings:
Maria Lewis, Countess of Dysart (d.1804) by John Constable (1776–1837), after Sir Joshua Reynolds. Painted in 1823. Constable stayed several times at Ham and became intimate with the family. He copied other portraits for them and in allusion to such tasks wrote in 1812: *I am making sad ravages of my time with the wretched portraits I mentioned to you. I am ungallant enough to be alluding to the Ladies' portraits.* (C.R. Leslie, *Memoirs of the Life of John Constable*, ed. Hon. A. Shirley, 1937, p.54.)

Pier-glass bearing the Tollemache family crest; mid-18th century.

53

Pier-glass and table decorated with floral marquetry, c.1680.

YELLOW SATIN DRESSING ROOM

The stone chimneypiece dates from c.1610.

Furniture:
The armchairs, dating from about 1760, are remarkable in that they are still upholstered in the original woollen cut velvet – a material particularly susceptible to attack by moths. The other chairs date from about 1780.

Inset painting:
Landscape with Classical Ruins by D. van den Bergen (1640–95).

Hanging paintings:
Capt. the Hon. John Tollemache (1748–77). Artist unknown.

Lyonel Robert Tollemache (1774–93). Artist unknown.

Lady Frances Tollemache (1738–1807), by Daniel Gardiner (1750–1805).

Louisa Manners, Countess of Dysart (1745–1840). Artist unknown.

Chimneypiece, c.1610, with late Victorian grate.

THE MUSEUM ROOM

Formerly a bedroom, this room has long been set aside as a museum room, where adequate protection from light, dirt and general wear-and-tear can be given to the rich collection of rare textiles.

THE MINIATURE ROOM

The important collection of miniatures on show in this room dates mainly from the 17th century but also includes a portrait of Queen Elizabeth I by Nicholas Hilliard and *An Unknown Man against a Background of Flames* by Isaac Oliver. Many of the miniatures can be recognized in the *Estimate of Pictures* of c.1679, which is also displayed here.

Queen Elizabeth I by Nicholas Hillyard.

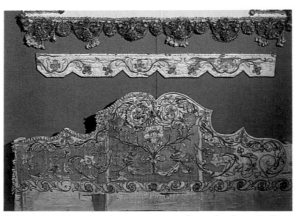

Bedhead and inner and outer valance from the State Bed, c.1680.

THE ROUND GALLERY
(FORMER GREAT DINING ROOM)

Up to about 1690 when the floor was pierced and the balustrade set up round the opening, this was the Great Dining Room, which formed, with the North Drawing Room, Long Gallery and Green Closet, the sequence of State Rooms of the 1630s (extended by the Lauderdales in the 1670s). These rooms were redecorated and furnished by William Murray in 1637/38 in the fashionable Court taste of the period, the leading exponent of which was Inigo Jones. Some decorative paintings were provided by Franz Cleyn, who worked for several other courtiers and was familiar with Jones's style. It is possible that he brought a measure of co-ordination to the whole enterprise at Ham, supervising the work of all the important tradesmen who contributed to the new scheme – mostly men who are known also to have worked for the Crown. (See Peter Thornton and Maurice Tomlin, 'Franz Cleyn at Ham House', *National Trust Studies*, 1980.)

The fine ceiling, cornice and frieze, in the style of Inigo Jones, are the work of Kinsman, the plasterer. The room is decorated in the original colour scheme of *fair blue* (as it was called in the bills), picked out with gilding. In William Murray's time there was a fireplace facing the windows and, at the end of the room where the high-table would have stood, a bay window at each side. The need for a great ceremonial dining room waned in the late 17th century and the room was therefore turned into an additional picture gallery.

As this guidebook was going to press, plans were in hand to hang tapestries on the walls of this room, in place of those that were here in the 17th-century: on the south wall, late 17th-century Flemish tapestries after paintings by Nicolas Poussin in the Louvre, depicting incidents in the life of Pyrrhus, King of Epirus, during the 3rd century B.C.; on the end walls, panels of Mortlake tapestry woven about 1675 and bearing the arms of the Duke of Lauderdale.

Detail of frieze and cornice in the Round Gallery.

Ceiling of the Round Gallery.

Furniture:
The pair of walnut sideboards probably date
from the 1650s and are recorded as having been
in this room in the 1670s.

The candlestands, described in the 1679
inventory as *Two Blackamore Stands*, are
probably Venetian.

Inset paintings:
Naked Boys with Lions by Franz Cleyn (1582–
1658).

Tobias and the Angel after the painting by
Adam Elsheimer (1578?–1610) at Frankfurt.
Probably by an artist of the Antwerp School.
About 1640.

Hanging paintings:
Frances, Lady Worsley (1673–1750). Grandmother
of Grace Carteret, Countess of Dysart. Attributed
to Charles Jervas (c.1675–1739).

Group of Gentleman on the Grand Tour,
attributed to Philip Wickstead (active 1763–
c.1790). The second figure from the left is said
to be 'Mr Tollemache' – probably Captain the
Hon. John Tollemache, R.N.

Wilbraham, 6th Earl of Dysart, as a Boy. Artist
unknown.

Lieutenant-General Thomas Tollemache
(c.1651–94 the Duchess's younger son) by Sir
Godfrey Kneller (1645–1723).

An Unknown Youth, attributed to Sebastien
Bourdon (1616–71).

Elizabeth Dysart, Duchess of Lauderdale,
attributed to Sir Peter Lely (1618–80).

Elizabeth Dysart in Youth by Sir Peter Lely.
This portrait, one of the most notable in the
house, dates from the late 1640s. Silvery in tone
and romantic in conception, it is yet more
interpretive of character than most of Lely's
portraits of fashionable ladies and may certainly

be counted among his finest works (frontispiece).

John Maitland, Duke of Lauderdale. School of
Lely.

Mrs. Heneage. Mother of Henrietta Cavendish,
Lady Huntingtower. Attributed to William
Wissing (1656–87).

Frances Worsley, Lady Carteret (1694–1743).
Mother of Grace, Countess of Dysart. By Sir
Godfrey Kneller. About 1715.

'Both Ye Graces in one Picture', as the 1679
inventory lists the double portrait of the Duke
and Duchess of Lauderdale by Lely. Painted in
the late 1670s, only a few years before the death
of the artist, it presents a remarkable contrast to
the earlier portrait of the Duchess both in style
and characterization.

Duke and Duchess of Lauderdale by
Sir Peter Lely (1618–80).

NORTH DRAWING ROOM

This room, to which guests withdrew from the Great Dining Room, still retains much of its 1630s decoration, notably the fine plaster ceiling and frieze by Kinsman (for which he charged £35.4s.) and the Mannerist panelling and doorcases on the window side, made by Carter, the joiner. The marble chimneypiece also dates from the 1630s, although the twisted columns and overmantel are believed to have formed part of the Great Dining Room chimneypiece, having been brought in here when the opening in the floor of that room was pierced (see p.101). These striking architectural features are attributed to Franz Cleyn, whose connection with this room is established by the 1683 inventory, where the inset paintings are attributed to 'Decline' – a variant of his name.

It is significant that the twisted half columns flanking the fireplace are copied direct from a work with which Cleyn was very familiar – Raphael's cartoon of the healing of the lame man at the temple gate, part of the famous *Acts of the Apostles*, which were acquired by Charles I and many times served as a model to the weavers at the Mortlake tapestry works, where Cleyn was artistic director. (Raphael's cartoons, which are the property of H.M. The Queen, are on loan to the Victoria and Albert Museum.) The tapestries seen here now were not hung in the room until the beginning of the present century. They are woven of silk and wool by ex-Mortlake weavers, perhaps at Soho and can be dated between 1699 and 1719 from the arms of Lord (later Earl) Shelburne. The scenes are partly derived from the earlier Mortlake series of 'The Months' (which were themselves derived with modifications from Flemish originals) and are put together in rather arbitrary sequences as follows:

1. Milking: April.
2. Ploughing and sowing: September.
3. Sheep-shearing and hay-making: June and July.
4. Hawking and reaping: May and August.
5. Vintage: October.

1630s panelling in the North Drawing Room.

Detail of North Drawing Room chimneypiece.

59

Furniture:

The gilded chairs, carved with dolphins and dating from about 1670, are probably of French or Dutch origin; their original silk covers are a rare survival.

The cabinet veneered with ivory, which dates from the 1650s, was also in the room in 1679 and must at the time have been highly prized, owing to the large quantity of ivory that went into its making.

The carved and gilded candlestands with shafts in the form of twisted columns entwined with vines probably date from about 1640.

The brass fire-dogs originally stood in the Great Dining Room.

Paintings:

The insets above the chimneypiece and doors are attributed to Franz Cleyn (1582–1658; see above). Done in tempera on paper, they are rather dilapidated. The roundel over the door to the Green Closet is a copy of the head of Helen from Guido Reni's *Rape of Helen* in the Louvre.

Left: Part of the set of 'dolphin' chairs.

North Drawing Room.

The Green Closet. From S.C. Hall, *Baronial Halls and Picturesque Edifices of England*, 1848.

62

THE GREEN CLOSET

The tradition of cabinets of curiosities had been introduced into England in the time of Charles I and this room – one of the earliest – is a rare survival, dating from the 1630s. Its walls, according to the 17th-century inventories, were covered with more than fifty miniatures and small paintings, for which *Green Sarsnet Case Curtaines* were provided as a protection against daylight.

Furniture (as listed in the 1679 inventory):
One ebony table garnished with silver. This table probably dates from the 1650s;[1] the fine embossed silver mounts are embellished with the letters ED for Elizabeth Dysart and a countess's coronet.

    Two Japan Cabinets and frames. These Japanese lacquer cabinets date from the 1630s.

    Two Squobb frames, two seats upon them covered with green damask, and green sarsnet cases. This entry refers to the long stools; a squab was a heavily stuffed cushion forming a seat.

    The silver-mounted mirror was probably in the North Drawing Room in the 17th century, when it must have hung over the wall-hangings.

The Green Closet.

Ceiling paintings:

The paintings by Franz Cleyn that decorate the cove and ceiling are done in tempera on paper and may well first have served as cartoons for tapestries. The same subjects with the same backgrounds occur in two panels of tapestry at Hardwick Hall, Derbyshire, woven at Hatton Garden some 20 years after Cleyn's death. Like the insets in the Marble Dining Room, they are based on 16th-century paintings by Polidoro Caldara. The figures in these paintings probably inspired the stands for the furniture.

Hanging paintings:

The following paintings were all here in the 17th century: *Boors Playing at Cards* by Pieter Verelst (c.1618–c.1678). Signed and dated 1653.

The Virgin and Child with St John the Baptist by Jacques Stellaert, also known as Stella (1596–1657). French School.

Danäe and the Shower of Gold after Hans Rottenhammer (1564–1625).

Landscape with Playing Boys and Goats, signed by Bartholomeus Breenbergh (1599/1600–?1656).

Salome with the Head of St John the Baptist by Stellaert; signed and dated 1637.

Bacchanalian Scene, attributed to H. van Balen (1575–1632).

Boors Smoking and Drinking after Adriaen Brouwer (1606–38).

Also displayed here are three portraits after Daniel Mytens (c.1590–before 1648):

Ludovick Stuart, Duke of Lennox and Richmond (1574–1624).

James, 2nd Marquess of Hamilton (1589–1625).

James I and VI.

Ceiling of the Green Closet by Franz Cleyn.

THE LONG GALLERY

The room was remodelled in 1639, when the present panelling with Ionic pilasters was installed by Carter, the joiner. His bill includes the items: *wainscott that was taken asunder and new made and all the mouldings of the wainscott at 4s the yarde £36.0.0. new work with the pedistalls 72 yards at 6s the yarde £21.12.0. 20 palasters of my one (own) stuff £10.0.0.*

This handsome panelling forms a splendid background for the set of Sunderland picture frames, richly carved with auricular ornament, which were supplied in the early 1670s by John Norris, 'frame-maker to the Court'.

Detail of panelling in the Long Gallery.

Long Gallery.

Furniture (as listed in the 1679 inventory):
One black ebony Cabinet and frame. About 1670.
(The doors have been removed to show the interior.)

Four Squobbs with Cases of purple and white Sarsnet. These seats, of about 1635–40, have traces of japanned decoration on their legs.

One Indian Cabinet with a gilt frame carved. This refers to the handsome Japanese lacquer cabinet, the stand of which may well have been made by Dutch craftsmen. About 1675.

Seavon boxes carv'd & guilt for tuby roses. About 1679. Six survive.

One table and stands of Inlaid marble. Described in an earlier inventory as being of 'counterfeit marble'. The table has not survived but the octagonal tops of the present 18th-century candlestands are of scagliola, or imitation marble, and presumably survive from the 17th-century originals.

Duchess of Lauderdale with a Black Servant by Sir Peter Lely (1618–80).

Charles II, School of Lely, above a Japanese lacquer cabinet.

Two great Globes and two small Globes. The terrestrial and celestial globes seen here now are signed Johan Senex and date from about 1730, so are probably replacements by the 4th Earl.

Paintings:
Duchess of Lauderdale with a Black Servant by Sir Peter Lely (1618–80).

William, 2nd Duke of Hamilton (1616–57) attributed to Cornelius Johnson.

Self-portrait after Van Dyck. The artist is shown pointing to a sunflower with one hand, while with the other he displays the gold chain bestowed on him by Charles I, apparently identifying himself with the sunflower and thus illustrating allegorically his devotion to the King. Several versions exist.

Called the *Countess of Southampton*. Artist unknown.

Lucy, Countess of Carlisle (1599–1660). Celebrated for her beauty and political intrigues. During the Commonwealth she lived at Petersham, where according to a contemporary 'she enjoyed herself more in this Retiredness than in all her former Vanities'. After Van Dyck.

Called *Ann, Countess of Bedford* (d.1684) by Sir Peter Lely. This identification is no longer accepted.

Margaret, Lady Maynard (d.1682; the Duchess's youngest sister) by Sir Peter Lely.

Catherine Bruce, Countess of Dysart (d.1649; the Duchess's mother). Artist unknown.

Elizabeth Tollemache, Duchess of Argyll (d.1735; the Duchess's elder daughter) by Sir Peter Lely.

Catherine Tollemache, Lady Doune (the Duchess's younger daughter). Artist unknown.

Sir John Maitland, 1st Baron Maitland of Thirlestane (1545?–1595. Lord Chancellor of Scotland; grandfather of the Duke of

69

Lauderdale). Dated 1589. Artist unknown.

Charles I (1600–49). Studio of Van Dyck. There are several versions. This one was probably given to William Murray by the king, as indicated in a note in a Memorandum of pictures bought by the king from Van Dyck, dated 1638–39, which reads 'le Roi vestu de noir a Monr Morre' (doubtless a French variant of Murray).

Colonel John Russell (one of Charles I's officers in the Civil War. After the Restoration first colonel of the First Foot, now Grenadier Guards. A member of the Sealed Knot). By John Michael Wright (1617–94); signed and dated 1659. A Scot by birth, Wright was one of the few native artists of real individuality and technical accomplishment among the host of foreign portrait painters who practised in England under the Stuarts. This is one of his finest portraits.

The Long Gallery about 1900. From Mrs Roundell, *Ham House, its History and Art Treasures.*

Called *Lord Allington.* The sitter is now, however, believed to be John Murray, Marquess of Atholl (1631–1703). School of Lely.

? *Sir Charles Compton* (d.1661; a prominent Cavalier leader) by Lely.

The Duke of Lauderdale in Garter Robes. School of Lely.

Charles II. School of Lely.

Thomas Clifford, 1st Baron Clifford of Chudleigh (1630–73; Lord Treasurer 1672; a member of the Cabal). After Lely. Versions by the artist are at Ugbrooke and Cirencester Park.

Called *Lyonel Tollemache, 3rd Earl of Dysart* (1648–1726; the Duchess's eldest son). The sitter is now believed, however, to be John Leslie, 7th Earl and 1st Duke of Rothes (d.1681), who became Chancellor of Scotland. By Lely.

Sir William Compton (d.1663. Brother of Sir Charles and like him a distinguished Cavalier commander. Second husband of Elizabeth, sister of Sir Lyonel Tollemache, 3rd Bt. A member of the Sealed Knot.) By Sir Peter Lely. There is another version in the National Portrait Gallery.

Colonel John Russell by John Michael Wright.

70

THE LIBRARY CLOSET

Furniture:

Linen chest, veneered with walnut; about 1675.

Cabinet on chest-of-drawers; about 1675. Probably two pieces of furniture joined together at a later date and fitted with new feet.

Bow-backed Windsor chairs. Mahogany; about 1760.

Paintings:

Two portraits of unknown ladies, one dated 1653. (Probably members of the Lauderdale family.) Artist unknown.

Inset paintings by Bega from rooms on the second floor.

THE LIBRARY

The Library and Library Closet were among the rooms added to the house by the Lauderdales. The change of style is clearly seen in the ceiling, which, instead of being divided into compartments by heavy bands of plasterwork, as in the earlier State Rooms, is lightly ornamented with a central wreath of laurels, surrounded by panels of delicate foliated sprays. The plasterer, Henry Wells, in his bill dated 1674, charged for *25 yards of frettwork in ye library at six shill. six pence ye yard.*

Henry Harlow, the joiner, supplied the book-shelves and window and door frames and also *the seder table with drawers In My Lords Librarie* at a cost of £12. The steps date from about 1740.

Though small, the Library once contained many rare books, including works printed by Caxton and Wynkyn de Worde. The Duke was a learned man and collected many valuable works; the 3rd Earl added many more important books. The collection was sold in the 1930s.

71

The Library desk.

ANTECHAMBER TO THE QUEEN'S BEDCHAMBER

In 1679 the walls were hung with green silk and velvet and the room was known as the Green Drawing Room. By 1683 it was designated the *Anti-roome to ye Queen's Chamber* and the present wall-hangings had been installed, framed with blue velvet decorated with appliqué embroidery and panelled with *blew Damusk* (now faded to a brownish colour; the survival of such hangings for three hundred years is quite exceptional).

Detail of wall-hangings in the Antechamber.

Furniture:
Cabinet veneered with strips of incised Oriental lacquer on stand of gilded pine. About 1679.

Japanned chairs, similar to those seen in the White Closet and Duchess's Private Closet; about 1675.

Screen of Oriental incised lacquer; about 1675.

Japanned close-stool; about 1679. This would have been kept in the closet behind the concealed door in the 17th century.

Miniature cabinet, Chinese, 17th century, with gilded stand added at a later date.

Inset paintings:
Landscape with a Man leading an Ass (over the fireplace).

A Lion Hunt and *A Landscape with Ruins* (over the doors). All by Dirck van den Bergen.

Hanging paintings:
Orpheus Charming the Animals, after Jacopo Bassano (1510–92).

Queen Henrietta Maria (1609–69), after Van Dyck. This painting formed part of the summer furnishings of the Queen's Bedchamber in 1679.

Classical Ruins with the Figures of Christ and the Woman of Canaan by Bartholomeus Breenbergh. Signed and dated 1635.

Classical Ruins with the Figures of Christ and the Woman of Canaan by Bartholomeus Breenbergh, 1635.

Antechamber to the Queen's Bedchamber.

THE QUEEN'S BEDCHAMBER

From this room, which was prepared for a visit of Queen Catherine of Braganza, one can see how the grounds are disposed symmetrically around an axis which passes straight through the middle of the room, stressing its importance as the culminating room in the sequence of State Rooms on this *piano nobile*. A model of the room as it must have looked around 1680 can be seen downstairs and a photograph of the model is displayed here.

The Queen's bed stood on a raised *parquet* (which was hived off from the rest of the room by a carved balustrade) at the far end of the room, facing the oncoming visitor. Inlaid into the parquetry, at the foot of the bed and on either side, are the cipher and ducal coronet of the Lauderdales. Made by Henry Harlow at a cost of 35s a square yard, the parquet was described as *Cedar inlaid wth wallnutt tree*; it was protected with *Two leather Covers for the stepp*. It was lowered to the level of the rest of the floor when the room was converted into a drawing room but the raised foot-walk, which is necessary to protect it, does suggest the higher level, which continued into the next room.

The plasterwork of the ceiling is similar to that

75

Detail of the Queen's Bedchamber ceiling.

The Queen's Bedchamber.

Model of the Queen's Bedchamber as it was in 1680.

in the last room but the treatment of the floral scrolls in the spandrels is more accomplished, with lively figures of men and animals among the foliage. The 1673 bill from the carver, John Bullimore, lists each section of the decorative woodwork. For the 6 *festons and a crown over ye chimney* he charged £6.10s. The gilding of the same festoons and coronet by Nicholas Moore cost £5.10s.

The chimneypiece, with its striking red and white streaked marble, also survives from the 1670s, together with the silver-mounted chimney furniture. The Lauderdales' cipher and coronet appear on the fire-pan and again on the silver mounts of the bellows (which are now displayed in the West Passage).

The Queen's Bedchamber was converted into a drawing-room by the 4th Earl. In May 1744 he paid George Bradshaw, the upholsterer, for the set of tapestries, which are similar to a set he supplied for Holkham, Norfolk. The subjects are made up from figures and motifs taken from pictures by Watteau and Pater. They portray:

The Dance.
The Fountain.
The Swing.
The Fruit-gatherer.

Furniture:

The console-tables and pier-glasses were supplied by Bradshaw at the same time as the tapestries.

The suite of chairs and a sofa, of similar date, are upholstered in red and green figured velvet, probably made at Spitalfields.

The harpsichord is dated 1634 and bears the name of the celebrated maker, Johannes Ruckers of Antwerp, but it is possible that it was made in London around 1730. 17th-century Flemish harpsichords, particularly those made by Ruckers, were in great demand on account of their excellent musical qualities throughout the 18th-century. Makers in London and Paris commonly adapted these by then ancient instruments to the extended musical requirements of their day and this harpsichord, with its spurious inscription, appears to be masquerading as a stretched instrument of this kind, although it may have been entirely new when acquired.

Paintings:
The Virgin and Child with St John after Andrea del Sarto (1486–1530). This is a copy of the once famous Pinti Madonna, which has itself been destroyed.

A Landscape and *A Pair of Lions with a Leopard in a Den* by Dirck van den Bergen (1640–95).

Pier-glass and console-table in the Queen's Bedchamber.

THE QUEEN'S CLOSET

This was a private room beyond the Queen's Bedchamber, to which only the most intimate friends of the Queen (or the Lauderdales) would have been admitted.

The ceiling is a smaller version of those in the bedchamber and antechamber but is painted to imitate marble and picked out with gold, while the oval panel contains a painting of Ganymede and the Eagle, which is attributed to Verrio. The carver's bill itemises all the decorative details, including *1 sheild* costing £1 and *1 cherubims face* costing 10s.

The original hangings of brocaded satin, described as *crimson and gold stuff, bordered with green, gold and silver stuff*, are extremely rare survivals of the most luxurious form of wall decoration of the period.

The fireplace surround is of scagliola and is perhaps the earliest example of this form of decoration in England. The ducal coronet and cipher appear once again in the design and also in the floor.

Furniture:
The armchair, covered in its original silk *en suite* with the wall-hangings, is one of the pair described in 1679 as *2 sleeping chayres, carv'd and guilt frames, covered with crimson and gould stuff with gould fringe* (the other is now shown in the Museum Room). Note the gilded ratchets for adjusting the angle of the back. Such chairs have become extremely rare but the Duke possessed others, as did Charles II.

The stools are probably the *Two small squob frames carv'd & guilt* that were in the bedchamber in the 17th century.

The little Chinese screen with painted silk panels may be the one that was in the room in 1679.

Inset paintings:
Three views of a *Mediterranean Seaport*, based on Naples, by Thomas Wyck (1616–77).

Hanging painting:
The Duke of Lauderdale by Cornelius Johnson (1593–1664?). (Incorrectly inscribed at a later date.)

Having completed the tour of the principal rooms, the visitor may, by returning to the Great Hall, visit some of the service areas.

Cipher and ducal coronet in the floor of the Queen's Closet.

The Queen's Closet.

THE WEST PASSAGE

An exhibition relating to the history of the house is shown here, while a wall-case contains a number of small decorative objects. On the wall above are the original leather fire-buckets.

Silver-gilt medal depicting the Duke of Lauderdale, 1672.

Group of cups and other decorative objects.

Cover of prayer book presented to William Murray by Charles I.

THE GENTLEMEN'S DINING ROOM

This room was the dining-room for the upper servants (who were classed as 'gentlemen') and now houses a small exhibition about the grounds of Ham House, including a model, as well as a model of the Queen's Bedchamber as it appeared in 1680.

THE BACK PARLOUR

This was the common room for the senior servants. The built-in oak cupboards, installed about 1679, are a notable feature of the room.

The English commode of about 1770 is in the French style and has affinities with the work of Georg Haupt and Christopher Fürlohg, who had come to England from Paris about 1767.

The Back Parlour.

THE BASEMENT

This is reached by way of the staircase at the far end of the West Passage. A booklet about the restored 17th-century kitchen is obtainable at the entrance desk.

Kitchen, showing the fireplace and stewing stove.

Kitchen, showing the dresser and shelves.

THE GROUNDS

The entrance gateway on the North Front was erected in 1671 to the designs of Sir William Bruce, cousin of Elizabeth Dysart. The stone was brought by water from Longannet Quarry on the Firth of Forth. It is recorded in the painter's bill of 1673 that the gates were painted blue and partly gilded. At that time a straight stone path led from the front door and continued in the form of an avenue leading to a landing stage on the riverbank. The forecourt was completely enclosed by walls, broken only by the entrance gateway, and *38 heads of lead*, as they were called in the 1679 inventory, were inserted in ovals in these walls. These busts, surfaced to look like stone, include representations of Charles I and Charles II, with a number of Roman Emperors and their ladies.

Twenty-two still remain in their original positions but the rest were resited by the 6th Earl shortly after his succession in 1799, when he took down parts of the forecourt walls in order to create the present gravel terrace. The sixteen busts thereby displaced were inserted in ovals in the front of the house itself, where they remain today. The pineapples along the terrace date from this time and are made of Coade stone, an artificial stone invented in 1769 and made at Lambeth. The same material was used for the figure of a River God, which is based on a bronze by John Bacon, R.A., at Somerset House. Coade's catalogue of 1784 advertises *A River God, 9 feet high, with an Urn through which a stream of water may be carried (100gns.)*. Under the arcades, which have always

Coade stone River God.

Carved oak bench, c.1675.

Detail of oak bench.

The garden at the east end of the house was known in the 17th century as the Cherry Garden, the trees possibly having been trained on the side walls. It has been restored to the layout shown on the plan of c.1671, with formal beds of lavender or santolina, edged with box and surrounded by yew hedges. The arbours at either side are of hornbeam.

Below the terrace on the South Front are eight grass squares, round which tubs and pots of plants would have been set out during the summer months. The original paths, which were laid out about 1673, were surfaced with gravel dug from Richmond Park. (Robert Smythson's plan of c.1610, p.90, shows that this area was already formally laid out at that early date, with the house situated on the axis. Sir Roy Strong comments that this was the earliest example of its kind.) Beyond lies the Wilderness, an area of grassy walks in the form of a *patte d'oie*, a popular feature of late 17th-century gardens, as practised by André Le Nôtre in France. This area is planted with field maples and hornbeam hedges. In the central clearing are modern reproductions of the chairs that stood here in the 17th century (see pp. 86–87). The originals, based on the Italian *sgabello*, may have been designed by Franz Cleyn (see Peter Thornton and Maurice Tomlin, 'Franz Cleyn at Ham House', *National Trust Studies*, 1980). Also here in the 17th century were eight statues, including copies of the *Venus de Medici*, Giambologna's *Mercury* and several *British Worthies*. Summerhouses have been built within four of the hedged enclosures, reproducing those to be seen in an engraving of 1739 (p.103), and wild flowers have been introduced to these areas. The central axis on which the house is sited continues across the central clearing and through the South Gates in a formal avenue leading to Ham Common. The three gateways on this side of the house were

been known as the Cloisters, are *Two carv'd wainescot benches* with splendidly carved armrests, that were listed as being there in 1679.

The restoration of the gardens on the east and south sides of the house to their 17th-century appearance was begun by the National Trust as a contribution to European Architectural Heritage Year 1975. They have been stocked with plants that are typical of 17th-century gardens and indeed many of them are known to have been grown at Ham.

The East Gates.

The South Gates.

Overthrow of the South Gates.

erected in 1675/6 and two still retain their imposing wrought iron gates. On the overthrow of the South Gates are the Tollemache coat of arms and motto, NEMO ME IMPUNE LACESSIT (No man can harm me unpunished).

Passing through the gateway in the west wall the visitor enters the Ilex Walk, with its statue of Bacchus, dating from 1672. The site of the former kitchen garden is now a rose garden, at the end of which stands the Orangery, part of which now serves as a tearoom. The three rather unusual trees in front of it are a Judas Tree (*Cercis silaquastrum*), a Western Red Cedar (*Thuya plicata*) and a Christ's Thorn (*Paliurus spinachristi*). More recent plantings include a black walnut, a mulberry and a number of pear trees.

Behind the Orangery and facing Ham Street lies the Stable Block, dating from the 17th century but altered and extended in 1787. (It is in private hands and is not open to the public.)

Facing the back of the Stable Block is the entrance to the Ice-House, built about 1800. Ice could be stored here until the summer, packed with straw, in the pit below the wooden floor. The beautifully-laid brickwork of which the dome is formed, can be seen on the inside but the outside was covered with concrete during the last war in order that it would serve as an air raid shelter.

At the end of the formal avenue leading to Ham House from the Petersham Road stands a gatehouse built about 1900 in Neo-Jacobean style.

Previous page: The South Front from the Wilderness.

Above: The Ilex Walk. *Below:* Interior of the dome of the ice-house.

The house was built by Sir Thomas Vavasour, a minor official at the court of James I; the loyal inscription, *Vivat Rex*, together with the date, 1610, is carved on the front door. A contemporary plan of the house shows a typical Jacobean H-plan, with the central doorway leading into one end of the hall in the traditional mediaeval way. Instead of a bay window in the extruded corner, however, serving to light a high-table, the newly fashionable feature of a loggia occupied this position at either side (known at Ham as the 'Cloisters'). Above the front door was a frontispiece or projecting bay and turrets with ogee caps rose from the Cloisters at either side (see p. 92). The house was no doubt furnished in a manner befitting a man of Vavasour's standing, and the garden was laid out in a way that reflects familiarity with recent developments in garden-planning

in France.[2] Despite later alterations, a number of features within the house (mainly chimneypieces and panelling) still remain from this period.[3]

The house then passed into the hands of John Ramsay, Earl of Holderness, a favourite of the King's, who is remembered for the part he played in rescuing James at the time of the Gowrie conspiracy in 1610. In 1626 it became the residence and, in 1637, the property of William Murray, the son of the parson of Dysart, a village in Fife, and a descendant of James II of Scotland. Since childhood he had been a close friend of Charles I and later came to belong to that inner circle of connoisseurs and collectors of art known as the Whitehall Group, that surrounded the monarch. Bishop Burnet (in the *History of his own time*, 1715) claims that he was 'very insinuating, but very false, and of so revengeful a character that

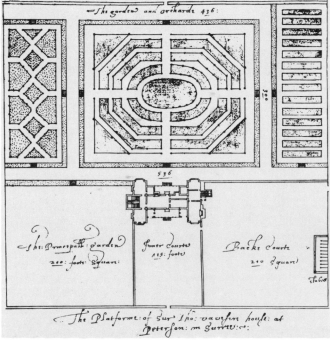

Robert Smythson's plan showing the layout of the house and grounds in about 1610. (RIBA).

The Cloisters.

The North Front as built. (Detail from a miniature by Alexander Marshall.)

William Murray, 1st Earl of Dysart, by David Paton (worked c. 1660–1695).

rather than any of the counsels given by his enemies should succeed he would have revealed them and betrayed both the King and them', and that 'he had one particular quality, that when he was drunk, which was very often, he was upon a most exact reserve, though he was pretty open at all other times'; this view is almost certainly biased, however. Murray was at any rate a man of refined tastes in matters of art, whose keen judgment led to his acquiring many excellent pictures and to furnishing himself with elegant surroundings in the most advanced fashion of the time.

In Murray's day the family rooms lay beyond the Great Hall at the eastern end of the house, with the Parlour on the ground floor in the wing now occupied by the Chapel. On the floor above, the two principal apartments (presumably those of Murray and his wife) led off the staircase landing and beyond were the State Rooms (a dining room and drawing room, followed by the Long Gallery with a closet alongside). These four rooms survive relatively unaltered. The servants' quarters and subsidiary rooms lay on the ground floor at the other end of the house, in the basement and on the top floors.

When Murray acquired the house in the 1630s its interior decoration must have seemed old-fashioned to someone familiar with the schemes then being created within court circles by Inigo Jones, schémes strongly influenced by contemporary French fashion. He therefore did over the interior in 1637 to 1639, employing leading artists and craftsmen, including the painter and designer, Franz Cleyn, who may have co-ordinated the enterprise, and Mathew Goodricke, who was responsible for the decorative paintwork.[3] Both had worked for the Crown so this refurbishing of Ham, much of which survives, no doubt reflects current court taste in interior decoration. During this phase the Great Stairs were rebuilt and the

State Rooms were entirely redecorated.

An inventory made shortly after the Civil War probably reflects the state of the interior arrangements when the redecoration had been completed; it indicates that the house was most fashionably appointed with co-ordinated colour schemes in which the wall-hangings, window-curtains, chair-coverings and table-covers all matched, producing a unified effect. The window-curtains were even divided in the modern way – a startling innovation at that period. The Green Closet housed many of Murray's smaller pictures and a superb collection of miniatures; although most have had to be removed for security, the room still conveys some idea of how a fashionable room looked in the time of Charles I.

Murray was created Earl of Dysart but when he died (c.1654) he had no male heir and the house was inherited by his daughter Elizabeth, who succeeded to the title of Countess of Dysart in her own right. She seems to have done a certain amount of refurnishing in the 1650s and 1660s,[3]

Elizabeth, Countess of Dysart, in her Youth. By Lely.

bringing the State Rooms up to date. The sideboards with caryatid supports, the silver-mounted table, the ivory cabinet and two portraits of her by Lely date from this period.

Contemporary chronicles testify to Elizabeth Murray's charms as a young woman. Already in 1644, when she was about eighteen, Henry Knyvet wrote to his wife[4] that he had come to know the Murrays well and that 'the eldest daughter is a jewel, and indeed a pretty one but for her deep coullerd hayer. I knowe not how such a notion would relish but 'tis sayd she is like to be a very great fortune.... Indeed, sweet Hart, such a pretty witty lass, with such a brave house and state as she is like to have, m'thinks might make a young 'fellow think her hayer very beautifull. I could find in my hart to wooe her for my sonne, for I am much in her favore. She seems to be a very good harmless vertuouse witty little bable'. Even Bishop Burnet, who was not among her admirers, admitted that she was 'a woman of great beauty' but that she was 'of far greater parts; had a wonderful quickness of apprehension, and an amazing vivacity in conversation; had studied not only divinity and history, but mathematics and philosophy; but what ruined these accomplishments, she was restless in her ambition, profuse in her expense, and of a most ravenous covetousness; nor was there anything she stuck at to compass her end, for she was violent in everything – a violent friend, and a much more violent enemy.' Yet the concern she showed for her children's welfare and her kindness to friends in trouble are evidence that she had a gentle side to her character.

About 1647 she married Sir Lyonel Tollemache, 3rd Baronet, of Helmingham Hall in Suffolk and he thus became the founder of a long line of Tollemaches who, as Earls of Dysart, succeeded each other at Ham House for nearly three hundred years. Unfortunately he lacked the ruthless ambition which his wife expected of her husband and, long before his death in 1669, she had formed a close friendship with the Earl of Lauderdale, a man whose ability and thirst for power made him a more suitable partner for a woman of her disposition. Lady Dysart had in fact to wait two more years before Lady Lauderdale died; whereupon she promptly married the widower. In the words of a contemporary,[5] 'Lady Dysart had such an ascendant over his [Lord Lauderdale's] affections that neither her age, nor his affairs, nor yet the clamour of his friends and the people, more urgent than both of these, could divert him from marrying her within six weeks of his Lady's decease'. The wedding took place on 17th February 1672.

The same writer asserted that Lauderdale 'really yielded to his gratitude, she having formerly saved his life by her mediation with the Usurper' (Oliver Cromwell). Bishop Burnet insisted that 'Cromwell was certainly fond of her, and she took care to entertain him in it, till he, finding what was said upon it, broke it off'. She must anyway have had some influence over Cromwell or it is unlikely that she could have lived with such freedom at Ham during the Commonwealth. There is also evidence that suggests Lauderdale was not the only royalist whose release from captivity she was instrumental in securing. Indeed, she probably never forgot that she was the daughter of the late King's close friend and she did much to help the royalist cause, being a member of the Sealed Knot, a secret society that worked for the King's restoration. Portraits of two members of that organization are still to be seen in the Long Gallery.

THE LAUDERDALE PERIOD

Elizabeth Murray, Countess of Dysart, married John Maitland, Earl of Lauderdale in 1672. Shortly afterwards he was created Duke and she thereafter assumed the superior title of Duchess although she was evidently proud of her Dysart heritage and its connection with Ham since she was to retain many reminders of her own family's standing even when she and husband altered and enlarged the house, a process that was started in 1672 and occupied several years.

Lauderdale was born in 1616, and began his career as a leader of the Scottish Covenanters; but towards the end of the Civil War, having formed a firm and lasting friendship with the future Charles II, he abandoned that cause and went over to the Royalists. He was with Charles at the Battle of Worcester, where, less fortunate than his master, he was captured by the Parliamentarians, who held him prisoner until the Restoration. Once released, Lauderdale soon re-established his favoured position with the King. Until his retirement two years before his death in 1682, the Duke remained closely associated with the King and his policies. He was a member of the so-called Cabal Ministry, a small and informal association of ministers forming an inner cabinet behind which Charles governed the country for a period. Lauderdale was also appointed Secretary for Scotland, in which post he assumed almost vice-regal powers, setting himself up in splendid state in the great Baroque extension he caused to be added to Holyrood House. With no other ministers responsible for Scotland, and provided that he followed the King's policies, he was allowed a free rein to run the country as he pleased.

Judging by his portraits, the Duke was not a

John, Duke of Lauderdale, by Edmund Ashfield (active c. 1670–1700).

prepossessing man but he was able, energetic and intelligent. Burnet, who knew him well but was a hostile witness, described him as someone who 'made but an ill appearance. His stature was large, his hair red, his tongue too big for his mouth, and his whole manner rough and boisterous, and very unfit for a Court. His temper was intolerable, for he was haughty beyond expression to all who had expectances from him, but abject where himself had any; and so violently passionate that he oftentimes, upon slight occasions, ran himself into fits like madness. His learning was considerable, for he not only understood Latin, in which he was a master, but Greek and Hebrew; had read a great deal of divinity, almost all historians both ancient and modern; and having besides an extraordinary memory, was furnished with a copious but very unpolished way of expression. The sense of religion that a long imprisonment had impressed on his mind was soon erased by a course of luxury and sensuality, which ran him into great expense, and which he stuck at nothing to support; and the fury of his behaviour heightened the severity of his ministry, and made it more like the cruelty of an Inquisition than the legality of justice.... He was the coldest friend and most violent enemy that ever was known'. Another commentator claims he was ever 'uttering bald jests for wit, and repeating good ones of others, and ever spoiled them in relating them, which delighted the good King much.... Besides tiring the King with his bald jests, he was continually putting his fingers into the King's snuff-box, which obliged him to order one to be made which he wore with a string on his wrist, and did not open, but the snuff came out by shaking. The King did some of his court honour to dine or sup with them, and a select company, agreeable to his pleasant and witty humour. This Lord although not invited ever intruded himself.'[6]

In Scotland, Lauderdale's policy was at first conciliatory but then became increasingly severe. Ruthless methods were employed against his for-mer friends the Covenanters. Some said the change from leniency became particularly marked after his marriage to Lady Dysart in 1672. The biased Bishop Burnet wrote that 'The Earl of Lauderdale had acted with much steadiness and uniformity before, but at this time there happened a great alteration in his temper, occasioned by the humours of a profuse, imperious woman.... After her hus-band's death she became so intimate with him, and gained such an ascendant over him, as much lessened him in the opinion of the world. For all applications were made to her; she sold places and disposed of offices, and took upon her not only to determine everything of this nature, but to direct his private conduct likewise, and as conceit took her would make him fall out with all his friends.' A contributory cause of his harshness and ill-temper was undoubtedly his deteriorating health, especially the pain caused him by a kidney disease. Moreover, carrying out the King's policies against the constant opposition of a great number of his countrymen cannot have been easy.

By her marriage with the Duke of Lauderdale, Elizabeth Dysart had become a power in the State and bore herself accordingly. Burnet records that 'they lived at a vast rate, but she set everything to

The South Front from the Wilderness by Henry Danckerts, c.1675.

sale to raise money, carrying herself with a haughtiness that would have been shocking in a queen'. The couple took up residence at Ham House, although they also had a house in Westminster and an apartment at Windsor Castle – as well as the new wing at Holyrood, and several lesser houses in Scotland, of which Thirlestane Castle was the most important.

Although Elizabeth Dysart had introduced some new furnishings in the 1650s and 1660s, the house must still, in 1672, have appeared very much as it had when the re-decoration carried out by her father had been completed in 1639 or so. To the newly-wedded Lauderdales it must have seemed out of date and was probably also too small for the kind of life that an aristocratic family now expected to enjoy. Such feelings would have been reinforced by what the Countess had seen during a visit to Paris in 1670. Indeed, she was apparently thinking of modernizing and extending the house already in 1671, before her marriage to the Duke. She consulted her cousin, Sir William Bruce, who was an extremely competent architect favouring the French style and was soon to become Surveyor-General of the Royal Works in Scotland and therefore responsible for the sumptuous extension of Holyrood for Lauderdale's occupation. It was decided almost to double the accommodation at Ham by building new rooms along the South Front, thus engulfing the wings. The proposals are illustrated in two watercolour drawings dating from about 1671 and attributed to John Slezer, a German engineer and surveyor also employed by Lauderdale at Thirlestane Castle, and the Dutch artist, Jan Wyck. The building work was carried out by the gentleman architect William Samwell between 1672 and 1674 with only minor alterations to the original proposals.

The painting by Henry Danckerts in the White Closet shows the South Front soon after the

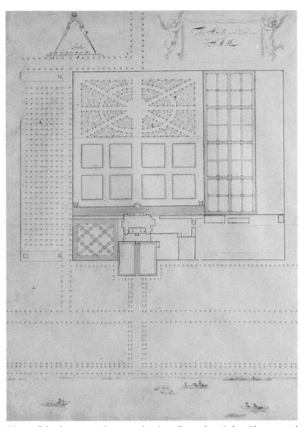

Plan of the house and grounds. Attributed to John Slezer and Jan Wyck, c.1671.

97

Drawing of the South Front. Attributed to John Slezer and Jan Wyck, c.1671.

Overleaf: The North Front.

work was completed. Sash windows were fitted in the new rooms and these were made to resemble the Jacobean ones, with their mullions and transoms, that were retained at the ends of the wings. An early 18th-century writer, praising the alterations at Ham, made this interesting comment on the retention of the bay window, a feature that had long been out of fashion: *The deformity (as now it is esteem'd) of Compass windows, is so disguised either with ye furniture within wch reduceth all to a square, or els by birdcages, and such Conceits without ... that it appears to No offence.*[7] Since then the Jacobean bays have been rebuilt in a later style and all the old window frames have been replaced with sashes of the familiar type. On the North Front the tops of the turrets were removed so as to give a continuous roofline right round the building.

It was particularly on the interior of the house that the Duke and Duchess now lavished their substance. The provided themselves with an apartment each, disposed symmetrically on either side of the new family dining room, which was built on the axis passing through the centrally-placed front door. The extensions to the State Apartment on the floor above made it possible to site the new State Bedchamber athwart this same axis. With the garden re-orientated so that the principal garden now lay to the south, the axial plan was further stressed out-of-doors. From the garden one could at a glance locate the principal room in the house – the State Bedchamber, on the principal floor of the building. Such an arrangement was an important feature of Baroque planning.

The interior was now decorated in a sumptuous manner and *furnished like a Great Prince's*, as John Evelyn put it. The State Rooms of the Murray period were redecorated and both they and the rooms in the new extensions were provided with new hangings and furniture. An inventory of the contents was made in 1677 when the refurnishing was largely completed. A second inventory was made in 1679 and a third in 1683, after the Duke's death. These give a very clear idea of how the rooms looked at this period, especially as so many of the contents still remain.

The Lauderdales employed mostly English contractors on this extensive re-furbishing of their Thames-side villa.[9] But Lauderdale mentions in a letter of 1673 'the two Dutchmen, who are excellent joiners… who made the shapies and lyneings of my rooms at Ham'. In another letter he calls them German but this is probably due to confusion on his part, and adds that they 'have wrought much for the finishing of this house, and have made the double chassees for the windows; in a word they are sober fellows, understand English enough, and most excellent workmen, both at that trade and for making cabinets'. Several closets were in fact fitted with double glazing ('double chassees', or double sashes, *chassis* meaning a frame in French). The cabinets for which these craftsmen were responsible were probably items like the built-in desk in the Library. Most of the furniture proper that was provided at this time was probably acquired from London tradesmen although the Lauderdales are known to have purchased several pieces of furniture from Amsterdam in 1672.[10]

The painted ceiling in the White Closet can confidently be ascribed to Antonio Verrio (1639?–1707), an Italian, who had come over from Paris where he had worked on royal commissions and was thus familiar with the style of decoration evolved by Charles Le Brun. (Other ceilings in the house, notably that in the Duchess's Private Closet, are attributed to Verrio himself or to his studio.) Verrio carried out important commissions for the English crown (e.g. at Windsor Castle and Hampton Court Palace); the Lauderdales no doubt frequently employed artists and craftsmen who had worked for the Crown since, being members of the inner Court circle, they would have been familiar with the latest exercises in interior decoration and furnishing at the royal palaces. Another example of his practice was the employment of the Dutch painter, Willem van de Velde the Younger (1631–1707), who came over to England for a short period during which he worked for Charles II. Not long after this painter's arrival in this country, the Duke had no less than four paintings by this artist set into the panelling of his bedchamber at Ham. The Duke, incidentally, patronised several of the Dutch painters who were active over here, many of these works being specially commissioned to be set into the panelling where they constitute an interesting and instructive series of paintings conceived as part of a decorative scheme. No less than fourteen are by Abraham Begeyn (called Bega: 1637–77) and a similar number by Dirck van den Bergen (1640–95). Others are by Thomas Wyck (1616–77) and his son Jan (1640–1702). The Lauderdales, themselves Scots, furthermore employed a Scottish painter named William Gowe Ferguson (1632/3–after 1695) to execute other furnishing pictures, notably those in the Private Closet which show Classical antiquities lit in a rather startling manner.

After the Duke's death in 1682, the Duchess stayed on at Ham. She had from the outset occupied the Bedchamber which had been prepared for the Duke and now seems to have taken over his Closet and Antechamber (Dressing Room) which were adjacent to that Bedchamber. She thus appropriated as her own the whole of what had been the Duke's Apartment. In later years the Duke's Closet came to be called 'the Duchess of Lauderdale's' and was preserved as such until late in the 19th century. One could still see there his 'sleeping chair', which she had subsequently used (she suffered badly from gout in her old age), and her

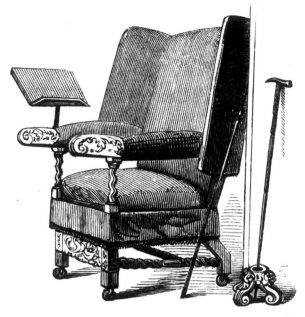

The Duke of Lauderdale's 'sleeping chair'. From S.C. Hall, *Baronial Halls and Picturesque Edifices of England*, 1848.

101

walking stick, as well as the canopy which was suspended over his chair. She made various other changes in the 1680s and 90s including, we believe, the conversion of the old Great Dining Room on the first floor, now that state banquets had gone out of fashion, into a second Picture Gallery, which enabled her to open up the ceiling in the Hall. It is possible that this work was carried out in 1688 for in that year William III landed in England and recommended the ousted James II 'for the greater quiet of the City and for the greater safety of his person that he doe remove to Ham, where he shall be attended by the Guards who will be ready to preserve him from any Disturbance'. James rejected the proposal on the pretext that 'Ham was a very ill winter house, and now unfurnished'. In fact, the house can hardly have become run down so quickly and we know that the Duchess was still living there (although she was taking the waters at Bath when this incident occurred). It may on the other hand be that many rooms had had to be closed while the opening up of the Hall ceiling was being carried out.

The Duchess of Lauderdale died in 1698 and was succeeded by Lyonel Tollemache, 3rd Earl of Dysart, her son by her first marriage (she had no children by the Duke). His mother's extravagances had left the estate encumbered and there was need of careful management. The economies practised by the new Earl were drastic in the extreme, however, and were continued long after they had ceased to be necessary. 'The frugal and sparing way of living which his circumstances at first made necessary hath habituated him to that which, now he is out of those circumstances, is downright stinginess', wrote a contemporary.[11] 'He suffered his daughters, like Roses, to fade ungathered because he can't find in his Heart, while he lives, to give them a Fortune worthy of their Birth.' His son, who died before him, was kept in such ignorance and so short of money that he only consorted with 'rascally Footmen and Domesticks, lolling whole days out of an upper Window with one of the Former for his Companion, playing Tricks and laughing for their Diversion at those who passed along'.[12] All this was especially surprising as he had possessed himself of a great fortune in marrying an heiress, Grace Wilbraham, and the estates he had inherited from his parents were very extensive indeed. Ham was thus allowed to deteriorate sadly from its former splendour during the 3rd Earl's tenure. 'The gardens are still well kept, but the House more neglected than one could expect from so great an Estate' was a comment made in 1724.[13] An inventory made in 1728 confirms this statement, for many items are then described as being old, while much furniture was piled in the attics. It must be added, however, the 3rd Earl was a bibliophile and significantly enlarged

Lyonel Tollemache, 4th Earl of Dysart, by John Vanderbank (1694–1739).

the important library which the Duke had founded at Ham.

When Lord Dysart died in 1727 he was succeeded by his grandson, also Lyonel, who became the 4th Earl. He married Grace, the daughter of the Earl of Granville, in 1729. In June 1730 a survey was made of Ham House which describes the state into which the house had fallen.[14] The bay-windows were said to be 'entirely ruinous and incapable of Repair otherwise than by Re-

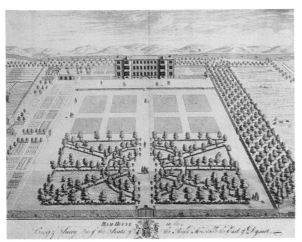
Bird's-eye view of the house and grounds. From an engraving published in *Vitruvius Britannicus* in 1739.

building them, and the sooner this is done the better'. The frontispiece above the front door was 'drawn off from the Wall, from the bottom to the Top ... it has gone so far as to endanger even pulling the Roof after it ...'. Presumably the urgent repairs were put in hand shortly afterwards. The 4th Earl's account books also record several large payments to James in the 1740s, presumably covering the rebuilding of the bays on the garden front, with Venetian windows above. A good deal of new furniture was acquired by the 4th Earl, notably the chairs, console-tables and pier-glasses supplied by George Bradshaw for the drawing-room he created out of the former Queen's Bedchamber. Unfortunately no inventory survives describing the rooms in the 4th Earl's time but a few bills survive and a certain amount can be inferred from the inventory of 1844.

The 4th Earl was succeeded by the 5th (yet another Lyonel) in 1770. He married Charlotte Walpole, a niece of Horace Walpole's who lived across the river at Strawberry Hill. A Reynolds full-length portrait of her hangs in the Hall. Of her betrothal, Walpole recounted 'Vidit, Venit, Vicit ... the young Lord has liked her some time;

on Saturday se'nnight he came to my brother and made his demand. The Princess did not know him by sight, but did not dislike him when she did; she consented, and they were to be married this morning'. According to Walpole she told her sister that 'If I was but nineteen I would refuse point blank. I do not like to be married in a week to a man I never saw. But I am two-and-twenty. Some people say I am handsome, some say I am not. I believe the truth is that I am likely to be large and go off soon. It is dangerous to refuse so great a match'.

Horace Walpole described the house as it was in 1770. 'I went yesterday to see my niece in her new principality of Ham. It delighted me and made me peevish. Close to the Thames, in the

Charlotte Walpole, Countess of Dysart by Sir Joshua Reynolds (1723–92).

centre of all rich and verdant beauty, it is so blocked up and barricaded with walls, vast trees, and gates, that you think yourself an hundred miles off and an hundred years back. The old furniture is so magnificently ancient, dreary and decayed, that at every step one's spirits sink, and all my passion for antiquity could not keep them up. Every minute I expected to see ghosts sweeping by; ghosts I would not give sixpence to see, Lauderdales, Talmachs, and Maitlands. There is an old brown gallery full of Vandycks and Lelys, charming miniatures, delightful Wouvermans, and Polenburghs, china, japan, bronzes, ivory cabinets, and silver dogs, pokers, bellows, etc., without end. One pair of bellows is of filigree. In this state of pomp and tatters my nephew intends it shall remain, and is so religious an observer of the venerable rites of his house, that because the gates never were opened by his father but once for the late Lord Granville, you are locked out and locked in, and after journeying all round the house as you do round an old French fortified town, you are at last admitted through the stable-yard to creep along a dark passage by the house-keeper's room, and so by a back-door into the great hall'. It was indeed difficult to gain access to Ham at this period. When George III, curious to see the celebrated old house with its many relics of an earlier Age, invited himself over from Windsor, his messenger returned with the reply from the 5th Earl that 'Whenever my house becomes a public spectacle, His Majesty shall certainly have the first view'.

A few pieces of good furniture from about 1770 are still to be seen in the house (notably the marquetry commode in the style of Christopher Fürlohg); it is likely that this was introduced soon after the 5th Earl's accession.

In 1799 the 5th Earl died childless and was succeeded by his brother, Wilbraham, as 6th Earl.

A Party in the Grounds at Ham House by Thomas Rowlandson (1756–1827).

Louisa Manners, Countess of Dysart by John Constable (1776–1837), after Hoppner.

He died in 1821 but during this period the interest in old buildings and their furnishings became more widespread and the Earl's antiquarian taste was reflected in 1813 when he had some Charles II chairs copied and covered in some 18th century red and yellow covers that had been stored away. He also adapted some bed-hangings *en suite* for a mahogany bedstead and installed this furniture in the Yellow Satin Room. The Neo-Jacobean oak frieze in this room probably dates from the same phase. John Constable stayed several times at Ham and was persuaded to copy portraits of members of the family; two of these pictures are still at the house. It was also in the 6th Earl's time that the forecourt was altered, when the pineapples and River God were introduced and some of the busts were set into the façade of the house itself (see p. 84).

With the death of the 6th Earl without issue, the Earldom passed to his only surviving sister, Louisa Manners. She died in 1840 and was succeeded by her grandson who became the 8th Earl. An inventory made in 1844 shows that many of the ancient furnishings were still in place. Much of it is described as being old and some of it as 'very old', and 'unfit for use'. The author of *Baronial Halls and Picturesque Edifices of England* (1848) wrote 'The Interior, with its gorgeous, yet remarkably tasteful "furnishing", has been scarcely altered since the aged dame [the Duchess of Lauderdale] occupied the Mansion'. In fact much of what she saw must have been the remains of the redecoration of around 1730 and it will have been this state which is reflected in the 1844 inventory. However, a certain amount of 17th-century furniture was also still very evident and the Duke's Closet, now renamed 'The Duchess of Lauderdale's Closet' (for, as we have explained, she had taken it over after her husband's death) was still preserved as a sort of shrine to the memory of this formidable lady. 'There still remain the chair in which she used to sit, her small walking cane, and a variety of objects she was wont to value and cherish as memorials of her active life and the successful issues of a hundred political intrigues.'

In 1879 Augustus Hare visited Ham and described this 'Sleeping Beauty' house[15] 'In the afternoon we went to Ham House – a most curious visit. No half-inhabited chateau of a ruined

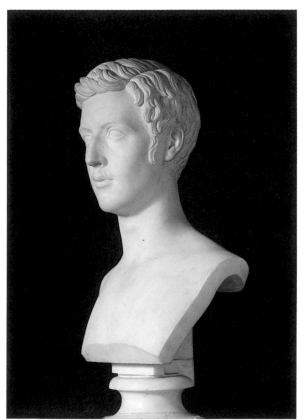

Sir William John Manners Tollemache, 9th Earl of Dysart. Bust by Alexander MacDonald, 1879.

family in Normandy was ever so dilapidated as this home of the enormously rich Tollemaches. Like a French chateau too is the entrance through a gateway to a desolate yard with old trees and a sundial, and a donkey feeding. All the members of the family whom I knew were absent, but I sent in my card to Mr. Algernon Tollemache, who received us. As the door at the head of the entrance-stair opened, its handle went through a priceless Sir Joshua of Louisa, Countess of Dysart: it always does go through it. We were taken through a half-ruined hall and a bedroom to an inner room in which Mr. Algernon Tollemache (unable to move from illness) was sitting. It presented the most unusual contrasts imaginable – a velvet bed in a recess backed by the most exquisite embroidery on Chinese silk; an uncarpeted floor of rough boards; a glorious Lely portrait of the Duchess of Lauderdale; a deal board by way of washing-stand, with a coarse white jug and basin upon it; a splendid mirror framed in massive silver on a hideous rough deal scullery table without a cover; and all Mr. Tollemache's most extraordinary huge boots and shoes ranged round the room by way of ornament', and 'We were sent over the house. All was of the same character – a glorious staircase with splendid carving in deep relief; the dismal chapel in which the different members of the family, amongst them Lady Ailesbury and Lady Sudeley, have been married, with the prayer-book of Charles I, in a most wonderful cover of metallic embroidery; marvellous old rooms with lovely delicate silk hangings of exquisitely beauti-ful tints, though mouldering in rags; old Persian carpets of priceless designs worn to shreds; price-less Japanese screens perishing; beautiful pictures dropping to pieces for want of varnish; silver grates, tongs, and bellows; magnificent silver tables, black chandeliers which look like ebony and are solid silver; a library full of Caxtons, the finest collection in the world except two; a china closet with piles of old Chelsea, undusted and untouched for years; a lovely little room full of miniatures, of which the most beautiful of all was brought down for us to examine closely. 'Do you see that mark?' said Mr. Tollemache. 'Thirty years ago a spot appeared there upon the miniature, so I opened the case and wetted my finger and rubbed it: I did not know that paint came off(!) Wasn't it fortunate I did not wipe my wet hand down over the whole picture: it would *all* have come off! Hare's des-cription was not published until 1900 by which time, as he said, 'Ham House has been greatly,

Ham House, Surrey. From a drawing by Henry Mogford, published 1845.

perhaps too much restored since this…'.

The restoration was carried out by Sir William John Manners, the 9th Earl, in the years following his succession in 1878. An inventory of 1884 records the state of the house before most of the work was carried out. Central heating was installed shortly after this; so was a new and complicated bath which may still be seen in the Bathroom originally created for the Duchess in the 17th century. The parquet floors in some of the principal rooms must also date from these renovations, when much of the ancient furniture was thoroughly restored.

Lady Sudeley, to whom Augustus Hare referred, described Ham in the *English Illustrated Magazine* of 1891, and claimed that the people portrayed in the Long Gallery paintings would find the room 'but little changed could they wake from their long sleep and enter it again in this latter end of the nineteenth century'. In fact there was about four times as much furniture in the Gallery in her time as there had been in the 17th century. She even believed that many of the old pieces of furniture were still 'in their ancient places'. This was actually true only with regard to the three closets, the Duke's, the Queen's and the Green Closet.

It was not until the 1960s that the Victoria and Albert Museum began to replace the ancient furniture in its original positions. The state of Ham House at the turn of the century is enshrined in Mrs Charles Roundell's *Ham House, its History and Art Treasures*, 1904. Its Sleeping Beauty quality then became renowned and the house for some while became the setting for social activities of all kinds. The house was described by Avray Tipping

Late 19th century view of the house.

in his *English Homes*, 1920, and illustrated articles appeared in *Country Life* and elsewhere. The 9th Earl died in 1935 and the house passed to his kinsmen, Sir Lyonel Tollemache, Bt, and Mr Cecil Tollemache, who generously presented it to the National Trust in 1948. The Trust in turn leased the house to the Ministry of Works (now the Department of the Environment), which maintains the building and grounds in close consultation with the Victoria and Albert Museum. The contents of the house were purchased by the Government and entrusted to the care of the Museum, which is also responsible for administering the house.

The Museum's policy in recent years has been as far as possible to recreate the house as it was in the 17th century – notably in its heyday under the Lauderdales – but also having regard for important earlier features and for later accretions. Where the original wall-hangings and chair-covers have not survived, reproductions have been made based as closely as possible on those described in the contemporary inventories, within the restrictions imposed by a limited budget and the choice of fabrics available today. In some rooms reproductions of 17th-century window curtains have been fitted to act as sunblinds but in others it has been necessary to exclude all daylight in order to protect the contents.

In 1975 the National Trust was enabled through benefactions to pay for the restoration of the 17th-century gardens (see p.85). It seemed right to restore the immediate surroundings of the house to their 17th-century appearance in order that they might form an appropriate setting for this outstanding 17th-century house. The garden made a great impression on John Evelyn when he visited Ham in 1678: 'After dinner I walked to Ham to see the House and Garden of the Duke of Lauderdale, which is indeed inferior to few of the best Villas in Italy itself; the House furnished like a great Prince's; the Parterres, Flower Gardens, Orangeries, Groves, Avenues, Courts, Statues, Perspectives, Fountains, Aviaries, & all this at the banks of the Sweetest River in the World, must needs be surprising.' Were Evelyn to return today he would not find Ham House and its gardens greatly altered.

Portrait of a Man, painted on a wooden panel; late 16th century, after Holbein.

SELECT BIBLIOGRAPHY

Thornton, P., and Tomlin, M., *The Furnishing and Decoration of Ham House*, published by the Furniture History Society, 1980.

Thornton, P., and Tomlin, M., 'Franz Cleyn at Ham House', *National Trust Studies*, 1980.

Thornton, P., 'Magnificence in Miniature – the Ham House Model', *Country Life*, January 26, 1978.

Thornton, P., 'Furniture from the Netherlands at Ham House', *Nederlands Kunsthistorisch Jaarboek*, Leiden 1980.

Tomlin, M., 'From Love-Seats to Firescreens – 18th century Furnishings at Ham House', *Country Life*, November 10, 1977.

Cornforth, J., 'Ham House Re-interpreted', *Country Life*, January 29 and February 5, 1981.

Dunbar, J., 'The building activities of the Duke and Duchess of Lauderdale, 1670–82', *Archaeological Journal*, vol. 132, for 1975.

Of interest also are:

Girouard, M., *Life in the English Country House*, London 1978.

Thornton, P., *17th century Interior Decoration in England, France and Holland*, New Haven and London, 1978.

Roundell, Mrs C., *Ham House, its History and Art Treasures*, London, 1904.

Cripps, D., *Elizabeth of the Sealed Knot*, Roundwood Press, Kineton, 1975.

Tollemache, Maj.-Gen. E., *The Tollemaches of Helmingham and Ham*, 1949.

FOOTNOTES

1 See P. Thornton and M. Tomlin, *The Furnishing and Decoration of Ham House*, published by the Furniture History Society, London, 1980, where the interior arrangements of the house are discussed in great detail.

2 See Sir Roy Strong, *The Renaissance Garden in England*, London, 1979, where it is suggested that the striking and, for England, novel axial garden plan was based on a knowledge of Claude Mollet's garden at St Germain-en-Laye, made for Henri IV.

3 See Peter Thornton and Maurice Tomlin 'Franz Cleyn at Ham House,' *National Trust Studies*, London, 1980.

4 B. Schofield, ed., *The Knyvet Letters*, 1949, pp.151–2.

5 Sir George Mackenzie.

6 Thomas Bruce, 2nd Earl of Ailesbury, *Memoirs*, Roxburgh Club, 1890.

7 British Museum, *Roger North Works*, vol. XIII.

8 See P. Thornton and M. Tomlin, *The Furnishing and Decoration of Ham House*, where the inventories are analysed in great detail and the surviving furniture is fully illustrated.

9 Arthur Forbes, builder.
John Lampen, mason.
Thomas Turner and William Smith, bricklayers.
Henry Wells, plasterer.
Thomas Gally, joiner.
Henry Harlow, joiner.
John Bullimore, carver.
Augustine Beare, glazier.
Nicholas Moore, painter and gilder.
Humphrey Owen, carpenter.

10 See P. Thornton, 'Furniture from the Netherlands at Ham House', *Nederlands Kunsthistorisch Jaarboek*, Leiden, 1981.

11 H. Prideaux, *Letters to John Ellis*, 20 July 1696.

12 Mrs Manley, *Secret memoirs and manners of several persons of quality*, 1709.

13 Mackey, *A journey through England*, 1724.

14 John James, *The Earl of Dysart's House at Ham in Surrey – upon a view taken thereof 16 June 1730*, Lauderdale papers, Buckminster Park.

15 Augustus Hare, *The Story of my Life*, 1900.

HOURS OF OPENING

All the year:
Tuesdays to Sundays inclusive, also Easter Monday,
Spring and August Bank Holidays, 11.00 to 17.00

Closed Mondays (except as above), 1 January, Good
Friday, May Day Bank Holiday, 24, 25, 26
December.

Children under 12 must be accompanied by an
adult.
Members of the National Trust are admitted free on
production of current membership cards.

TRANSPORT

Underground (District Line) or British Railways
(from Waterloo or Broad Street Station) to
Richmond Station; buses 65 or 71 to Fox and Duck
Inn, Petersham.

Guided tours of the house can be arranged. To avoid
congestion parties have to be limited to a maximum
of 30 people but more than one group can be taken
round at the same time if necessary. Application
should be made to the Education Department,
Victoria and Albert Museum, London SW7 2RL.

APSLEY HOUSE

THE WELLINGTON MUSEUM
149 Piccadilly, London W1

OSTERLEY PARK HOUSE

Osterley, Middlesex

APSLEY HOUSE, sometimes called 'Number One, London' was the home of the first Duke of Wellington, famous for his success in the Peninsula War, and later a leading statesman. He acquired the house from his brother Marquis Wellesley in 1817 and in the late 1820s employed Benjamin Dean Wyatt to create the present house, which encases the original brick house built by Robert Adam in the 1770s. The Duke's magnificent picture gallery contains paintings from the Spanish royal collection and among the many masterpieces displayed at the house are the Portuguese centrepiece and the Waterloo shield which commemorates his success at the Battle of Waterloo, 1815.

Open all year, Tuesday, Wednesday, Thursday and Saturday: 10.00 to 18.00. Sunday: 14.30 to 18.00.
Closed Good Friday, May Day Bank Holiday, Christmas Eve, Christmas Day, Boxing Day and New Year's Day.

There are regular guided tours, usually on Thursday at 13.00. Details of these and other talks can be obtained from the programmes issued by the Education Department, Victoria and Albert Museum, South Kensington, London SW7 2RL. Telephone: 01–589 6371, ext. 316 or 258.
Groups can obtain the services of a qualified guide lecturer through the Education Department, Victoria and Albert Museum as above.

OSTERLEY PARK HOUSE is a property of the National Trust, administered by the Victoria and Albert Museum.

An Elizabethan mansion transformed into an eighteenth-century villa with elegant neo-classical interior decoration designed by Robert Adam for the banker Robert Child. Osterley is remarkable in that it still boasts much of its eighteenth-century decor and retains its grand Georgian furnishings. The antechamber of the state apartments is one of the few rooms in the world to remain in its entirety as it was in the 1770s.

Open all year, Tuesday to Sunday inclusive, 11.00 to 17.00. Closed Good Friday, May Day Bank Holiday, Christmas Eve, Christmas Day, Boxing Day and New Year's Day. Open on other Bank Holidays.

Guided tours can be arranged through the Education Section, Victoria and Albert Museum, South Kensington, London SW7 2RL. Telephone: 589 6371; ext. 247 or 258.